WILD ORCHIDS OF MALLORCA

Nicole T. Beniston
William S. Beniston

WILD ORCHIDS OF MALLORCA

EDITORIAL MOLL
MALLORCA
1999

Primera edició: desembre 1999

© Nicole T. Beniston, William S. Beniston
© EDITORIAL MOLL
Torre de l'Amor, 4
07001 Palma de Mallorca

I.S.B.N.: 84-273- 0824-8
Depòsit Legal: PM. 2.457-1999

Imprès a Gràfiques Miramar, S.A.
Torre de l'Amor, 4
07001 Palma de Mallorca

WILD ORCHIDS OF MALLORCA

PART 1

FOREWORD

Orchids... The name usually brings to mind those flowers with gorgeous hues and fantastic forms that rank amongst the most glamorous and fascinating plants of the tropics. More rarely is the name associated with the Orchids of our own environment which, at various times of the year, grace meadows and scrub, woods and marshes, even banks along busy highways.

These are much humbler plants, of course, and few of them could boast the status of ornamentals. Yet, however small their flowers – and some are minute – their appearance, colours, markings and above all the peculiarities of their reproductive organs leave no doubt as to their close relationship to the tropical blooms, while their originality and complexity, together with the loveliness of most of them, cannot fail to arouse an interest tinged with wonder..

These discreet Orchids are intriguing plants indeed, and the more one learns about them, the more extraordinary they seem, so that, often, interest develops into a compelling passion ... A passion which leads to an endless quest combining the excitement of discovery with the satisfaction of unravelling some of the mysteries of nature through a bet-

One of the humblest Orchids: *Ophrys bombiliflora*

An Orchid as colourful and attractive as its tropical relatives: *Ophrys tenthredinifera*

ter understanding of these unique plants, amongst the most recent in terms of evolution and still in the process of evolving.

Orchid hunting is particularly rewarding in Mallorca, for, given its size, the island offers an impressive number of species, further increased by subspecies, varieties and hybrids. Besides which, since members of the Orchid family may be found during the greater part of the year except at the height of summer, the search for them provides endless aims for excursions which, in turn, give the opportunity to enjoy the diversity and beauty of the Mallorcan scenery in its seasonal variations.

Exciting as their discovery may be, however, Orchids are to be treated with the utmost respect, and temptation to pick them should be resisted. For they are extremely fastidious plants which require specific conditions in order to become established and most of them take several years (in some cases more than ten years) to progress from seed germination to flowering.

Their destruction, however caused, is therefore a lasting, often irreparable loss. Already their numbers have been sadly depleted and some species even seem to have vanished altogether, particularly in the recent past, as developers' bulldozers ruthlessly laid waste vast tracts of

Cala Tuent

Port des Canonge

Orchids' favourite habitats, especially along the island's coasts.

Fortunately, a radical change of attitude towards the environment has taken place in the Baleares. Mallorca's Orchids have benefited from it and have now been officially declared "protected species". A welcome decision, it is still too often overlooked, not only by the new generation of developers, but by excursionists and week-end picnickers who inflict damage upon the flora through ignorance or indifference.

Such plants as Orchids must be allowed to live and follow the slow course of their evolution. A better knowledge and appreciation of the various species commonly found in the island, all the more vulnerable for that very reason, is bound to help towards their survival and further progress ... Thus, it is hoped that this little guide will serve a useful purpose and a worthwhile cause.

INTRODUCTION

ABOUT ORCHIDS

The Orchids found in Mallorca, and indeed in all the Balearic Islands, represent but a very small proportion of the species comprised in the Orchid family, for these exceed 20000 most of them plants of the tropics – and while, until recently, only some 150 species were listed as terrestrial Orchids pertaining to the European and North African flora, this number has lately reached unsuspected heights, following the introduction of a new system of classification.

According to widely accepted theory, Orchids probably appeared in the Malayan archipelago more than 20 to 30 million years ago and are considered to provide one of the most sophisticated examples of evolution – as is obvious when studying in greater depths Orchid biology and ecology. It appears, moreover, that Orchids are still in the process of active evolution, although, amazing as they already are, one may wonder to what further lengths they can go to ensure their survival!

The name given to this vast family – Orchidaceae – has more prosaic origins than seems to befit such remarkable plants, for it derives from the Greek word "orkhis", meaning "testicle" and thus recalls the shape of the two tubers which characterise some of the most common Orchids of the Mediterranean region.

Given this resemblance, it is hardly surprising that aphrodisiac properties were long attributed to Orchid tubers. Nowadays, however, only the nutritive value of their contents is acknowledged – a fact which was recognised from early time in the Middle East, where the substance extracted from the tubers, known as Sahlep (or Salep), was used as the base of a winter drink and exported to European countries for the same purpose. But the days of the Sahlep drink have gone and terrestrial Orchids are of little economic use, unlike their exotic relatives which provide appreciable revenues for countries where breeding and growing Orchids has developed into a thriving industry.

West coast

One can only regret the relative lack of interest in the cultivation of terrestrial Orchids. Although on a much reduced scale, their flowers are as intricate, indeed as attractive as the blooms of their brilliant counterparts. Besides, cultivation would contribute to their preservation. For many are at risk in an environment where development often means encroachment on nature or simply wanton destruction.

GENERAL CHARACTERISTICS OF TERRESTRIAL ORCHIDS

However different they may seem, at a first glance, from their more showy relatives, terrestrial Orchids such as those found in Mallorca share with them all the features that distinguish Orchidaceae from other families. True, one or other feature may appear, singly, in plants from other families, but what sets Orchids completely apart is the way several features have combined to make the flower structure very special indeed.

Orchids, therefore, are very distinctive plants and thus easy to recognise, be it the humblest of them, at the peak of the Mediterranean spring, when flowers of all shapes and colours abound everywhere.

The plant

Terrestrial Orchids are herbaceous perennial plants, most species with tuberous roots, some with rhizomes.

The leaves are entire, usually alternate, the basal leaves mostly spread out, often forming a rosette, the upper leaves, generally of reduced size, sheathing the stem. As in all monocotyledons, the veins run lengthways and are more or less parallel.

The stem, single, bears a spike-like inflorescence.

The inflorescence comprises flowers of varied appearance according to genus and species, which have all one obvious feature in common, i.e. the lower petal, strikingly different from the other external parts of the flower. Each flower, in most species, is attached to the stem by what appears to be the stalk, but is in fact the ovary, often ribbed and twisted.

Bracts, i.e. leaf-like organs usually on a reduced scale and often colourful, are generally present at the base of the ovary.

The fruit is a capsule, i.e. a dry fruit, splitting open to release a large number of minute seeds, light as dust.

Example of Orchid: *Orchis longicornu*

Example of Ophrys: *Ophrys lutea*

Example of Orchid Flower: *Orchis robusta*   Example of Ophrys Flower: *Ophrys balearica*

The flower

The perianth

The perianth of an Orchid flower, i.e. the external non-reproductive organs, consists of six parts, arranged in two whorls

3 sepals, which form the outer whorl and are often alike
3 petals, which form the inner whorl, only two of which are alike, while the third and lowest petal known as the labellum or lip is very distinctive in size, shape, colour and texture.

In many cases, this labellum or lip is prolonged at the base by a tubelike appendage filled with nectar and called the spur.

In the case of the genus Ophrys (Bee Orchids), the labellum or lip bears a shiny patch or markings, known as speculum or mirror.

The two identical petals and the three sepals, especially the central one, often curve forward to form a kind of hood or helmet serving to protect the sexual organs

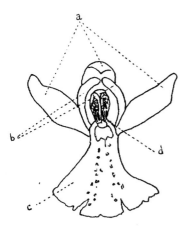

Fig. 1. Orchis flower (front view): a. sepals. b. petals. c. labellum or lip. d. column

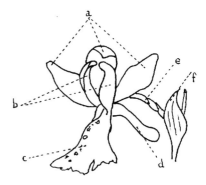

Fig. 2. Orchis flower (side view): a. sepals. b. petals. c. labellum or lip. d. spur. e. ovary. f. bract

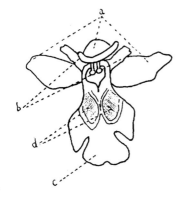

Fig. 3. Ophrys flower (front view): a. sepals. b. petals. c. labellum or lip. d. speculum or mirror

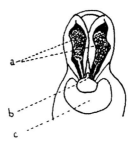

Fig. 4. The column: a. pollinia or pollen masses. b. rostellum (including bilobed bursicle). c. stigmatic surface

Fig. 5. Detail of pollinium: a. pollen grains. b. caudicle. c. viscidium

The column

In flowering plants of most families, the flowers have separate male and female organs. The male organs consist of stamens, which bear anthers containing pollen grains, while the pistil, i.e. the female organs, comprises the ovary, which is usually connected by the style to the stigma where pollen grains are deposited during the pollination process.

The Orchid flower differs from all others in combining the male and female organs into a single structure of great complexity, known as the column.

In most cases, only one stamen is present, comprising pollinia or pollen masses enclosed in membranous envelopes and set side by side.

Each pollinium or pollen mass contains thousands of pollen grains compactly held together by threads of a sticky substance.

Usually, a stalk or caudicle connects each pollinium to a sticky disc called viscidium which may be enclosed in a pouch-like flap or bursicle. There is no style or stigma recognisable as such. Instead, below the pollinia and central to the flower, a cavity contains the stigmatic area or areas where pollen is trapped during the pollination process.

A sterile stigma, the rostellum, is present in many Orchid flowers in the form of a projection – often beak-like – which is situated between the pollinia and the stigmatic area or areas and helps to prevent self pollination.

The ovary

In Orchidaceae, the ovary – containing the egg cells which, after fertilisation, develop into seeds – is situated below the flower.

In most cases, as has been mentioned, the ovary supports the flower, thus acting as the stalk. However, the real nature of this apparent stalk is eventually revealed and its function clarified for, soon after fertilisation takes place (in the wake of pollination), it starts to swell, gradually maturing into the fruit – a capsule – packed with seeds.

While the flower is at the bud stage, the labellum or lip is the uppermost petal, yet, when the flower is fully open, it may be observed occupying the lowest, most forward position ... What has happened?

The conjuror responsible for this incredible sleight of hand is – again, in most cases – none other than the ovary which, through a 180° twist, brings down to the fore this most important part of the flower, which will serve as a landing pad for potential pollinators

POLLINATION PROCESS

The structural features of Orchid flowers, so sophisticated, provide an unparalleled example of adaptation to insect pollination.

In the case of terrestrial Orchids, the most common insect pollinators are of the bee and wasp type, and it is interesting to note that specialisation is such that some Orchids are pollinated by a single species of insect. Hence the development of a whole set of devices to attract the right insects at the right time and ensure successful pollination, therefore survival – the ultimate aim. In some instances, the plants' strategy verges on science fiction!

First, the potential pollinator must somehow be lured to the flower. So, like many other flowers, Orchids bring into play fragrance and colour: individual scent may vary in intensity according to the time of day and the insect to attract; as to colour, variations on red frequently occur, since red seems particularly attractive to bees and their relatives, and often, when the main colour happens to be different, markings in red or purple act as signals to interested insects.

Form is equally important, as insects generally choose to visit flowers suitable to their body shape and size.

The lip of an Orchis flower with visible guide lines: *Orchis olbiensis*

Luring the insect to the flower is not enough, of course. It must be persuaded to alight and stay! This is where the labellum or lip plays its part, for this distinctive petal has been turned into a landing platform.

Once the insect has landed, it must be enticed to proceed further so that it may come into contact with the organs that matter – and what better enticement than reward in the form of food? Thus, like a large number of flowering plants, many Orchids produce the sweet nutritive substance known as nectar, usually and cunningly hidden in the spur – whenever the appendage, which also serves as advertisement, is present. In the absence of nectar, there may be other forms of reward to tempt

A flower with the appearance and texture of a female insect: *Ophrys speculum*

pollinators and, as will be seen later, none are as bizarre (and cruel) as the promises of bliss proffered by the deceitful "Bee Orchids" (genus Ophrys).

From the landing platform, then, the insect is led inside the flower, along a path defined by what appears to be coloured lines, spots or dots, but, in fact, generally consist of minute projections. Ridges or grooves may also be used as additional guide-lines.

As the insect reaches the centre of the flower, it runs into the column, normally hitting it with its head (with other parts of its body in one or two cases). Following the impact, the pollinia or pollen masses are dislodged and the sticky disc at the base, the viscidium, ensures they become firmly attached to the insect's head in the vertical position. Usually, however, within seconds, the pollen masses bend at a 90° angle until they reach the horizontal position, so that by the time the insect visits a new flower, the pollen is deposited on the stigmatic surface, thus enabling pollination to be carried out successfully.

Once pollinated, Orchid flowers lose their scent and wither, for there is no longer any need to advertise their presence, but as long as they remain unpollinated, the flowers keep blooming until, in desperation and as a last resort, some may practise self-pollination.

As for "Bee Orchids", a close look at individual flowers provides a clue to the pollination process, which is regarded as the ultimate in adaptation to insect pollination.

Adaptation through mimicry, this time ... For there is no doubt about it, "Bee Orchids" resemble insects! Sepals and petals combine to give the impression of an insect's body, bright or dull according to the species, hairy where it should be, its eyes gleaming, its antennae raised, its wings folded or spread out – an insect at rest or ready to take off...

In fact, the shape, colour, texture and even scent are apparently so realistic and alluring that male pollinators confuse these pseudo-insects with their own female partners and actually try to mate with them. In the process, they usually collect the pollen masses, which they deposit in the next flower they visit, eager as they are to repeat their attempt at mating in the hope of success. And so on...

There is more than mimicry, however, in this close association with insects and the mystery of such an extraordinary relationship deepened even further when it was discovered that, in most cases, "Bee Orchid" flowers bloom before the females of their insect pollinators have emerged!

Yet, this highly specialised adaptation, remarkable as it is, is nevertheless flawed, for quite a number of "Bee Orchids" rely on only one or two specific insects for pollination, with the consequence that, should the pollinator disappear or fail to materialise, for whatever reason, the plants are doomed to extinction.

LIFE CYCLE:
FROM SEED TO SEED

Once the seeds have been dispersed, terrestrial Orchids assume the appearance of all decaying herbaceous plants and soon few visible traces are left of their existence. Yet, this does not necessarily mean death. Often, life goes on underground.

In the case of many tuberous Orchids, for instance, by the time flowering takes place, one tuber has practically withered after exhausting its food reserves in the process of the plant's growth, but during this process, if conditions have been favourable, a new tuber has formed and is soundly embedded in the ground when the upper parts of the Orchid have disappeared. In due course, using the food stored in this tuber, a new plant emerges and the Orchid's life cycle starts all over again.

In this way, given suitable climatic and soil conditions, Orchids may ensure their survival for a number of years.

Meanwhile, hopefully, new crops of Orchids may issue from the tiny seeds, which the wind has carried off to fresh pastures. But that is no simple feat and a whole set of conditions must be met before success is achieved!

For the seeds are so small that they lack the reserves necessary for the plant to develop normally. Assistance to stimulate growth is therefore a prerequisite, but whence and how? The answer to this problem is provided by a certain fungus (or several fungi) encountered in the soil, with which Orchids may succeed in establishing a close partnership, known as mycorrhizal association.

Thus, in the course of germination (or prior to it according to some authors), fungus threads penetrate the Orchid seed, actively promoting the plant's development by supplying, through a very complex process, nutrients extracted from the soil. In return, it is thought that the fungus (or fungi) also derives some nutritious benefit from the association.

Ingenious as it may sound, such a partnership is not as straightforward as it appears, for if it is to be wholly successful a delicate balance must prevail in the "give and take" transaction. Any disturbance in the optimum pattern of mutually beneficial exchanges and the Orchid's growth is interrupted or delayed. Thus, at best, development is very slow, and years may elapse before survivors reach maturity.

Once the first leaves appear and allow photosynthesis to proceed, the Orchid plant is theoretically equipped to lead an independent life. Some Orchids do so, freeing themselves from their entanglement with the fungus (or fungi), others continue to rely on their associate to enhance growth at times of stress, and a few species simply cannot do without their fungal partner. Such is the case, for example, of the "Bird's Nest Orchid" (*Neottia nidus-avis*), a saprophyte plant whose pale flowering stems sometimes introduce a light note in the sombre shade of holm-oak forests.

When the flowering stage is reached, the Orchid's life-cycle draws towards its end. Following pollination, the ovules, in the ovary, are fertilised and gradually develop into seeds. Petals and sepals wither and the swollen ovary itself turns into a dry fruit (technically a capsule) whose hardened sides eventually split open, releasing the seeds which the wind then disperses, sometimes transporting them over great distances. Needless to say, there is much wastage on the journey and when seeds land on the ground, it is only with a good deal of luck that the Orchid life-cycle may start anew.

In view of the complexity of the process involved, it is obvious that a vast number of seeds are simply doomed to perish. Which explains why Orchids produce seeds in such profusion ... As another ploy to increase their chances of survival

HABITATS

Although some terrestrial Orchid species may be found in various habitats, most of them favour specific environments, where the type of soil, climate and surrounding vegetation provide the necessary conditions for their optimum development.

As regards soils, only a few Orchids show a preference for acid soils (i.e. siliceous soils or other soils deficient in humus and/or essential minerals) and there is no doubt that the majority of species flourish on basic soils with a high content of lime, for besides being soils rich in humus and minerals, they may also support more readily the fungus (or fungi) which plays such a vital part in Orchid growth.

The occurrence of species in different types of soil may, in some cases, reflect a suitable degree of adaptation, but may also point to the presence of significant quantities of lime in the soil or to the nature of the underlying strata. Generally speaking, though, soils may be used as a clue in the search for Orchids, and their partiality for calcareous (i.e. limy) soils explains their numbers and variety in Mallorca, especially in the lower regions of the "Serra de Tramuntana" mountain range, which is mainly limestone.

Of course, other factors intervene to determine the distribution of

Open pinewood (*Pinus halepensis*) where many species of Orchids are found

Holm oak woods at foot of Massanella

Neottia nidus-avis growing in decaying leaves in holm-oak wood

Orchids on the island. Thus, rock strewn terrain where the disappearance of forests has given rise to a new type of vegetation – often referred to as garrigue – characterised by scattered wild olive or oak-trees and evergreen bushes with grassy patches in between, provides a particularly favourable environment for Orchids (and other herbaceous perennials), which can obtain both the light or shade they require as well as humidity at the early stage of growth.

For similar reasons, the same species appear at the edge of the dense vegetation covering many hillsides, known as maquis – and in grassy clearings among pine woods, for the main species of pine in the island is the "Aleppo Pine" (*Pinus halepensis*) which also thrives on limestone.

However, a number of Orchids have their own requirements. Thus, while both the "Small Early Purple Orchid" (*Orchis olbiensis*) and the "Pyramidal Orchid" (*Anacamptis pyramidalis*), for instance, just seem to grow on grassy, sunny hillsides, the latter is usually found in longer grass and drier terrain. By contrast, species belonging to such genera as Limodorum (Limodore), Epipactis (Helleborine) and Cephalanthera (White Helleborine) shun bright sunshine and seek refuge in the shade of woods – pine woods in the first case, holm-oak woods in the other two. Holm-oak woods also shelter

Orchis olbiensis growing by Asphodels in the garrigue

the saprophyte "Bird's Nest Orchid" (*Neottia nidus-avis*), deeply embedded in decaying leaves. As to the rarest amongst Mallorcan Orchids, the handsome "Marsh Loose-flowered Orchid" (*Orchis robusta*), it is a plant of the wetlands which may only be seen in one or two places, in the midst of the giant reeds of the Natural Reserve of S'Albufera...

It should be noted that the conditions prevailing in these habitats and propitious for the growth of Orchids may easily be disturbed by all sorts of factors... The vagaries of the Mediterranean climate may wreak havoc on these plants and their environment, while grazing animals may cause irreparable damage to the associated vegetation.

However, man's activities often prove to be even more harmful, directly or indirectly: felling trees or cutting branches may destroy microclimates, the use of insecticides on a

---

NOTE: Although terrestrial Orchids may be found in many parts of Mallorca, hunting for them – for some at least – in a limited area may prove as fruitful as criss-crossing the whole island.

Thus, the South-west region is a very favourable terrain, with plenty of pine woods where grassy margins and clearings are often speckled with various species in full bloom, and with well exposed hillsides which harbour a whole range of Orchids, some on the wane, others in their prime.

However, perhaps as a consequence of urban and tourist development, a few species have vanished from the Southwest or remain very elusive. This is the case, in particular, of the rare "Yellow Bee Orchid" (Ophrys lutea), for which the best hunting-ground seems to be the Northeast region, more specifically the pine woods along the road linking Alcudia to Arta, where other species also commonly grow.

And, of course, there are the slopes of the "Serra de Trarnuntana" which offer great possibilities of discovery. It is a rather extensive area to cover, but, after all, much of the pleasure derived from the quest for Orchids lies in the quest itself and the excursions it occasions.

nearby farm may reduce the population of insect pollinators etc.

Hence, there is no guarantee that the healthy Orchids seen one year in a given habitat will reappear the next. They may have opted for a temporary absence ... or they may have vanished for good.

CLASSIFICATION OF ORCHIDS

The classification of plants poses many problems and botanists have rarely been unanimous in grouping and naming species. It is no wonder, therefore, that in the case of such complex plants as Orchids – plants, moreover, prone to variability and not averse to hybridisation – disagreement often arose concerning nomenclature. Hence, recently, a reappraisal of European Orchids based on new criteria.

As a result, at least one well-known species has been promoted to the status of genus (*Barlia robertiana* formerly known as *Himantoglossum longibracteatum* – the "Giant Orchid"); a number of subspecies have attained the rank of fully-fledged species and many species have been regrouped according to the closeness of their relationship (e.g. the *Ophrys sphegodes* or "Early Spider Orchid" group, the *Orchis tridentata* or "Toothed Orchid" group etc.) ; and whenever necessary new names have been devised or old ones

Mountain slopes, favoured by various species when well exposed

revived. In the particular case of the Balearic Archipelago, an attractive Ophrys, previously described as *O. bertolonii*, then as *O. bertoloniiformis*, has lately been declared an endemic species, to be known, henceforward, as *Ophrys balearica*.

Reappraisal continues and there remain undoubtedly enough subspecies, varieties and hybrids to give rise to new controversies or rekindle old arguments!

Needless to say, such developments do not contribute to the simplification of the amateur botanist's task as far as the accurate naming of Orchids is concerned. However, recent publications by specialists provide a reliable basis for identification and whenever there seemed to be consensus regarding changes in classification and names, the new status and/or name of the Orchids concerned have been adopted in the present volume (with former status and name(s) indicated in brackets).

Obviously, while changes in nomenclature, often based on very specialised research and involving subtle differences, are important, perhaps they remain of greater concern to specialists than amateur botanists, for whom much of the pleasure of Orchid-hunting lies in the discovery of these enchanting plants and their study at close quarters, together with the possibility of further investigation. Besides, whatever changes are taking or have taken place, the number of Orchids commonly found in Mallorca (with but a few exceptions) remains unaffected – a number quite remarkable in such a relatively restricted area, as will be appreciated from the list below.

Epipactis: Helleborine
    E. microphylla

Cephalanthera: White Helleborine
    C. damasonium
    C. longifolia

Limodorum: Violet Limodore
    L. abortivum

Neottia: Bird's Nest Orchid
    N. nidus-avis

Spiranthes: Lady's Tresses
    S. spiralis (S. autumnalis)

Gymnadenia: Fragrant Orchid
    G. conopsea

Neotinea: Dense-flowered Orchid
    N. maculata

Orchis: Ground Orchid
    O. longicornu
    O. fragrans var. martrinii (O. coriophora ssp. fragrans)
    O. conica (O. tridentata)
    O. lactea (O. tridentata ssp. lactea)
    O. italica
    O. olbiensis (O. mascula ssp. olbiensis)
    O. robusta (O. laxiflora ssp. palustris)

Aceras: Man Orchid
    A. anthropophorum

Barlia: Giant Orchid
    B. robertiana (Himantoglossum longibracteatum)

Wetlands, home of *Orchis robusta*

Anacamptis : Pyramidal Orchid
   A. pyramidalis

Serapias : Tongue Orchid
   S. lingua
   S. parviflora

Ophrys : Bee Orchid
   O. speculum (O. ciliata, O. vernixia)
   O. lutea
   O. fusca
   O. iricolor (O. fusca ssp. iricolor)
   O. dyris (O. omegaifera ssp. dyris)
   O. incubacea (O. sphegodes ssp. atrata)
   O. balearica (O. bertolonii, O. bertoloniiformis)
   O. apifera
   O. tenthredinifera
   O. bombyliflora

Other Orchid species, reported to be present in the island, are extremely rare and highly localised – thus necessitating an extensive knowledge of the terrain and a thorough search, unless an expert guide is available.

Still other species are mentioned in various botanical works on Mallorca, but these have not been found for decades and specialists regard their presence as very doubtful.

Note: In the section devoted to the description of individual Orchids, this standard botanical classification from *Flora Europaea* has not been followed, for, in order to assist Orchid-hunters in their quest, the plants are presented according to the season and month in which they tend to appear.

CONCLUSION

It is hoped that this introduction will prove of value, especially in the case of newcomers to Orchids, who, by now, may appreciate more readily why these plants, humble as they may seem at a first glance, are considered extraordinary – indeed, unique – and they may also experience the kind of fascination which sooner or later will send them on the Orchid trail and prompt them, perhaps, to seek more information.

Given the number of Orchidaceae in Mallorca, their wide distribution and various habitats as well as the different seasons in which they make their appearance, it is obvious that the island offers plenty of scope for discovery and enjoyment as far as these exciting plants are concerned. But there is much, besides, to be discovered and enjoyed : the autumn maquis, when "Strawberry Trees" (*Arbutus unedo*) are laden with brilliant fruit and clusters of creamy bells ; the garrigue in spring with the ground a bright patchwork of flowers, mountain slopes glowing in the sun, forests of "Holm-Oak" (*Quercus ilex*) filled with darkness and silence ... And often distant vistas truly magnificent.

Orchids also represent a fresh challenge to the keen photographer,

Delightful plants such as this *Ophrys balearica* are now officially protected, but protection needs to be ensured

A last glance at marvellous vistas after a day's Orchid hunting...

for, generally small and sometimes minute, they call for new techniques ... and a great deal of patience. Orchids make for wonderful close-ups and success in capturing their complexity and beauty is a reward well worth the effort.

Mallorca, then, is an ideal place to indulge in Orchid hunting – a pastime, or for some, a passion, which offers endless opportunities to learn more about nature and delight in its beauty. But nature is fragile and plants are especially at risk, for they cannot "run away" from immediate danger and are therefore at the mercy of any abuse. Hence, care must be taken not to harm them wantonly or damage their environment.

When the survival of such amazing plants as Orchids is in question, however, there is only one answer: official protection. This is a step which authorities in the Baleares have already taken. But to be effective, protection must somehow be ensured ... and what better deterrent against depredation than a greater awareness of the uniqueness of Orchids? The general public needs to be better informed – which is where this little volume may also prove of benefit.

WILD ORCHIDS OF MALLORCA

PART II

Spiranthes spiralis   Autumn Lady's Tresses
(S. autumnalis)

Around the Mediterranean shores, autumn is in many ways a second spring and among the plants suddenly flowering at this time of the year are those which survived the long summer drought thanks to the reserves stored in their underground organs. *Spiranthes spiralis* is such a plant. It may not be so conspicuous as the "Late Narcissus" (*Narcissus serotinus*) or the crocus-like "Merendera" (*Merendera filifolia*), for it is rather discreet and often seeks the seclusion of pine woods, but it sometimes forms quite showy little colonies and its tiny frilly flowers of a translucent white, curiously twisting around the stem, must count among the sweetest flowers of the Mallorcan autumn.

Spiranthes spiralis is a slender plant, 10 to 30 cm tall, with small bract-like leaves sheathing the stem.

These are new leaves, issued from new tuberous roots, which last throughout the winter and spring and wither long before the stem arises from their midst so that there is no evidence of the plant's presence during the summer.

The inflorescence is a dense spike of very small flowers spiralling around the stem and often arranged on the same side. Bracts are present, slightly longer than the stalk-like ovary.

The flowers are 5 to 6 mm long, white tinged with green, fragrant. There is no spur. While the 2 lateral sepals are often spread out, the median forms with the 2 petals a kind of tubular hood.

The lip is rounded at the tip and crinkled at the edges.

Glandular hairs are particularly noticeable on the stem, and on the ovary, bract and median sepal of the flowers.

Flowering: Generally from late September to November, but not always recurring yearly.

Habitat: A variety of soils and terrain, but the plant seems to favour small clearings in pine woods along the island's coasts. It does not seem to climb much above 600m.

Name: Both the generic and specific names originate from the Greek *speira* – a "coil" and refer to the striking appearance of the inflorescence, as does, in a more evocative way, the English name "Lady's Tresses". Seen from the back, the flowering spike is certainly reminiscent of plaited hair.

Note: The tubers were regarded as an aphrodisiac in ancient times, and in popular medicine, a tincture obtained from them was long used to alleviate skin affections and eye complaints.

Ophrys fusca   Sombre Bee Orchid

Just when the flowering spell of the Mallorcan autumn seems to be drawing to an end, as "Narcissi" and "Merenderas" have already vanished and in the woods the bright pinks of the heather are fast fading, *Ophrys fusca* suddenly appears. With its small dark flowers, it is not one of the most striking of Ophrys species and may easily be overlooked along the banks of forest tracks or in the garrigue grass where it fitfully grows throughout the winter.

However, with the advent of spring, Ophrys fusca becomes far more assertive and may be encountered in many parts of the island, together with two of its closest relatives – *O. iricolor* and *O. dyris* – which cannot fail to attract interest owing to the size of the first and the colourful markings of both.

Ophrys fusca is a plant of variable size usually reaching between 10 and 30 cm, with basal leaves forming a small rosette and one or two upper leaves, reduced in size, sheathing the stem.

The inflorescence comprises from 2 to 8 small, spurless flowers with bracts longer than the ovary which serves as stalk.

The 3 sepals are greenish to yellowish, the 2 lateral usually spread out, the median curving forward. The 2 linear petals, slightly wavy, may be edged or tinged with purplish brown.

The elongated lip, up to 1.5cm long, is 3-lobed, with the side lobes either well formed or hardly developed and the longer middle lobe indented. It is a deep velvety brown, generally thinly edged with yellow and the "speculum" consists of two bluey patches usually clearly outlined.

Flowering: Late November to end of April

Habitat: *Ophrys fusca* is one of the most common Orchids and flourishes in a variety of soils and terrain. It may be found on grassy hillsides or stony ground, in garrigue or in maquis, in pinewoods or along the roadside. It grows in mountains up to around 1000 m

Name: The generic name *Ophrys* is the Greek word for "eyebrow" and may refer to the shape, colour and texture of the petals or to the ancient use of these plants for dyeing eyebrows.
The Latin word *fusca*, meaning "dark", refers to the colour of the labellum or lip. "Bee Orchid" is the common English name of the genus and stems from the bee-like appearance of the flowers of another species: *Ophrys apifera*.

Ophrys iricolor was long considered a subspecies of *O. fusca*, then regarded as a species in its own right. Its presence is mentioned in several quite recent works on the Balearic Islands, but it should be noted that, according to the very latest research, the distribution of the plant now classified as *O. iricolor* seems to be limited to the eastern part of the Mediterranean region. Hence, the status of the handsome Ophrys described below remains debatable.

It appears in the spring and is a relatively impressive plant, with a flowering stem reaching up to 40 cm and quite large flowers. The resemblance to *O. fusca* in the inflorescence is obvious but the sepals are wider and green while the petals are a deep orange or reddish brown and have

distinctly crinkled edges. The lip, some 2 to 2.5cm long, with well developed side lobes, is particularly striking as the "speculum" gleams an iridescent blue (hence the specific name evocative of "rainbow-like hues") against the dark brown of the ground colour. There is no yellow margin, but the underside is often tinged with orangey yellow. Thrusting forward and with recurved edges, the lip offers a characteristic profile.

Ophrys dyris (from the Latin name of the Moroccan Atlas mountains) has experienced several changes. First classified as a subspecies of *O. fusca*, it came to be considered a subspecies of *O. omegaifera* when the latter was accorded the status of species. But, again, following new research, it seems that *O. omegaifera* is an eastern Mediterranean plant while *O. dyris*, which tends to be regarded as a full-blown species, is limited to the western part of the region.

Appearing in the spring, it is a slender plant which generally bears only a few flowers. However, these are rather attractive and a closer look reveals the petals with reddish margins and wavy edges, raised like antennae between the green dark-veined sepals, while, on the maroon ground of the 3-lobed lip, the lighter-tinted "speculum" stands out, glistening, hemmed by a whitish border recalling the letter W (or the Greek letter 'omega").

Barlia robertiana — Giant Orchid
(Himantoglossum longibracteatum)

A sturdy plant, *Barlia robertiana* is all the more noticeable as its fragrant flowers appear very early in the year, at a time when there is relatively little competition from other flowering plants along the forest margins and on the sunny hillsides where it is often found, sometimes in conspicuous groups, though it may also opt for the protection and shade of bushes in the garrigue.

While the dense flowering spike rising above shiny leaves immediately attracts interest, the first impression it conveys may be one of dullness, for the prevailing hues of greyish or purplish pinks tinged with brown and green are rather subdued, but there are exceptions to this lacklustre and brighter flowers are not uncommon.

A more striking form of this plant, rare but present in Mallorca – at least in the eastern region – has large creamy flowers whose lip is edged with green.

Barlia robertiana is a plant of robust aspect, which may reach some 50 cm and has large leaves, shiny and a light green, several of them erect around the stem.

The thick stem, often tinged purple, bears a dense spike of large fragrant flowers the colour forms (pale greenish pink or brighter and purplish) varying according to the plant. The spur is short, pointing downwards. The bracts are conspicuous, longer than the stalk-like twisted ovary.

The 3 sepals are greenish or brownish and purple-veined, the median curving forward to form, together with the 2 petals, a hood over the column, the lateral broad and cupped, often purple-spotted on the inside.

The lip, spirally twisted when in the bud, reaches 2.5 to 3cm, with the ground colour, purple-marked, paler than the wavy margins. It is 3-lobed, the side lobes well developed, sickle-shaped, the middle lobe divided and the two segments leg-like, with the result that the whole flower brings to mind a helmeted human figure.

Flowering: Early February to late April.

Habitat: *Barlia robertiana* is quite a common plant in Mallorca and seems to favour neutral as well as chalky soils. It thrives on sunny grassy slopes, as well as among garrigue shrubs and bushes or in pinewood clearings. It may even be seen on roadside banks and alongside tracks.

Name: The generic name was given as a tribute to the XIXth century French botanist Barla, while the specific name honours the XVIIth century botanist Robert, also French.

Orchis conica   Conical Toothed Orchid
(O. tridentata)

    A newcomer to the latest nomenclature, *Orchis conica* usually boasts to be the first member of the Orchis genus to flower on the island, sometimes as early as mid-February. Although it rarely reaches an impressive size, it is not a plant easily ignored, for it dots generously uncultivated terraces and woods alike with its dense spikes of flowers, white or pink and very dainty, reminiscent of little women in spotted skirts and beribboned bonnets whirling to the sounds of a vigorous tune!

Orchis conica is a plant of 15 to 25cm, with basal leaves spread out and upper leaves, reduced in size, sheathing the stem.

The inflorescence consists of a dense spike – conical or ovoid in shape – of small flowers, white to pink in colour, with the lip often raised and the curved spur pointing downwards. The bracts are membranous and the twisted ovary serves as stalk. The 3 sepals – white or pale pink, with a green base and purplish-green veins on the inner side – have elongated tips and form, together with the 2 linear petals, a hood over the column ending in three long curving points at the front.

The lip is only 5-8mm long, with the white or pink ground colour spotted purplish pink or purple. It is 3-lobed, with the side lobes oblong to flared, irregularly serrated at the edges and generally spread out, and the middle lobe entire or divided into two very shallow flared lobes, often irregularly serrated at the edges and with a small tooth in the centre.

There are variations in ground colour and the central spots may be so dense as to form a wide unbroken band.

Flowering: Mid-February to late April.
Habitat: This plant favours limestone and is quite common among grass on sunny hillsides and long-abandoned terraces, in grassy patches of garrigue and open woodland.
Name: Orchis, the generic name, is the Greek word for "testicle" and refers to the appearance of the two tubers from which many Orchid plants develop.
This species is characterised by the "conical" shape of the inflorescence.

Orchis lactea
(O. tridentata ssp. lactea)

    Scattered among the previous species and often confused with it, *Orchis lactea* or "Milky Orchid" is a plant with a sturdy stem rarely exceeding 20 cm in height, which bears a spike
of white to pale pink flowers with the lip usually purplish pink-spotted.
    However, this Orchid is characterised not so much by its colouring as by some specific features which may be observed in particular in the lip, which is somewhat convex, straight and narrow below the side lobes before flaring out. The side lobes themselves are generally recurved, widening towards the slanting serrated top edge, while the median lobe is often indented, sometimes bearing a small tooth in the middle.
    The spots, which often take the shape of "dashes", may be so dense as to form a continuous band.

Ophrys tenthredinifera   Sawfly Orchid

Ophrys tenthredinifera is regarded by many as one of the most beautiful Bee Orchids, not only for the size of its flowers, but for the range of shades within the colours of the markings: silvery blue or sombre tones of the modest "speculum", reddish or dusky hues of the central patch on the flared lip, wide border of a golden, sulphurous, greenish or rusty yellow – the whole gamut is astonishing, as is the striking contrast offered by the outspread sepals and petals which often are a brilliant carmine pink!

This very attractive plant is common in Mallorca, which apparently boasts some of its most handsome forms as well as a number of interesting hybrids.

Ophrys tenthredinifera is a plant reaching up to 35 cm, or more on occasion, with basal leaves forming a rosette and one or two upper leaves, reduced in size, sheathing the stem.

The inflorescence usually comprises between 2 and 8 spurless flowers, but more than 10 is not an uncommon occurrence, making the spike quite conspicuous. The bracts, green or greenish pink, are longer than the stalk-like ovary.

The 3 spreading sepals, large and broadly oval, vary from pale to bright pink and are generally prominently green-veined, while the small petals, of triangular appearance, are often en even brighter pink and, being hairy, seem velvety.

O. tenthredinifera bombyliflora

The lip, some 2 cm or so long, is more or less rectangular and usually has the two side lobes reduced to protuberances, whereas the indented middle lobe has a small yellowish appendage curving forward. A brown patch, quadrangular, partly spreads across the lip – with, at its base, the "speculum", entire, indented or divided – contrasting with the yellow or greenish border of variable width, which is softly hairy and may occasionally be reflexed instead of flared.

Flowering:	Mid-February to late April.
Habitat:	*Ophrys tenthredinifera* is mainly found in grassy clearings of pine woods and maquis, on stony, grassy hillsides and in the garrigue.
Name:	For the generic name *Ophrys*, see *Ophrys fusca* p. 36. As this Ophrys species is pollinated by a "Sawfly", a small wasp-like insect belonging to the *Tenthredinifera* family, the plant is said to be, literally, "Sawfly bearing".
Note:	*Ophrys tenthredinifera* apparently hybridises with several other "Bee Orchids", in particular with the tiny *O. bombyliflora*, which abounds in the island and is often found happily mixing with its relatives. The results of such cross-pollination are intriguing and it is quite exciting to try and identify the features which characterised the parent species.

Orchis longicornu   Long-spurred Orchid

One of Mallorca's most attractive Orchids, *Orchis longicornu* is a slender plant with a purple-flushed stem bearing a rounded spike of delightful flowers, which may vary from a subtle pink (or even white) to a much deeper hue, and look their prettiest when the folded wings of the lip are tinted a rich deep violet vividly contrasting with the fitfully spotted white centre.

With their long spur tilted up and uncommonly arched, they seem delicately poised, ready to take off at the slightest hint of alarm.

When this Orchid exceeds average size and its flowers reach their peak, it is quite an impressive plant.

Ophrys longicornu is a plant 15-35cm tall, with basal leaves forming a rosette and upper leaves, reduced in size, sheathing the stem up to the inflorescence. The inflorescence consists of a lax spike of long-spurred flowers, with purplish bracts about the same size as the twisted stalk-like ovary, itself purplish. The 3 sepals, pale or purplish pink and darker veined, form, together with the 2 smaller petals, a hood over the column, often almost horizontal.

The lip is 3-lobed, with the middle lobe shorter than the wide side lobes which are typically a dark purple and are usually reflexed so that the lip looks folded with the centre, generally white, dotted pink or purple.

The long spur, variable in colour, has a thickened tip and curves upwards.

Flowering: Late February to May

Habitat: Some of the best stands of *Orchis longicornu* are found in open pine woods and abandoned terraces – but these are under serious threat as the tall tough grass *Ampelodesma mauritanicum* is a ruthless invader of unattended terrain. The plant is also quite frequent in garrigue, where it tends to shelter under shrubs.

Name: For the generic name Orchis, see *Orchis conica* p. 42. *Longicornu*, borrowed from Latin, focuses on the main characteristic of this species: its "long horn-like" spur.

Ophrys bombyliflora   Bumble Bee Orchid

The smallest of the "Bee Orchids" to be found in Mallorca, *Ophrys bombyliflora* makes up for its diminutive size by growing in quite large colonies. Thus, seen from a distance, the tiny flowers, suitably shaped and coloured, could be mistaken for a swarm of miniature bees intent on gathering nectar – which is probably part of the stratagem these little plants developed in order to attract their pollinators.

Ophrys bombyliflora is known to hybridise with other species, in particular with *O. tenthredinifera*, hence offers possibilities for the discovery of fascinating crossed specimens in the vicinity of the parent plants.

While *Ophrys bombyliflora* occasionally reaches some 20 cm, it tends to remain in the 5-10 cm bracket.

As it produces several tubers at the end of roots, it soon forms dense and quite extensive colonies.

The basal leaves are rosetted, turning black as they decay.

The inflorescence is lax, comprising 1 to 4 or 5 flowers, with greenish bracts shorter than the rather long stalk-like ovary.

The 3 oval sepals, pale green with darker veins, are often fully spread

and the 2 tiny petals, greenish tinged with purple or brown at the base, hairy and almost triangular, are erect.

The lip, 4 to 7 mm in length, is 3-lobed, the side lobes densely hairy and hump-like, and the middle lobe rounded and convex, with a small appendage in-turned. The dark ground colour and the purplish or brownish "speculum" not very well defined, contrast with the rather pale sepals.

The gleaming "eyes" at the side of the large stigmatic cavity and the bright red tip of the column terminal projection are particularly striking.

Flowering:	Late February to May
Habitat:	*Ophrys bombyliflora* commonly occurs in open pinewoods and grassy, stony areas, with a preference for short grass.
Name:	For the generic name *Ophrys*, see *Ophrys fusca* p. 36.
	The specific name includes two Latin words: flora i.e. "flower" and bombylis i.e. "silkworm" (as it turns into a chrysalis), thus referring to the shape and soft hairiness of the side lobes of the lip.
	The common English name is said to recall the resemblance of the flower to a small "Bumble Bee"

Ophrys incubacea   Black Spider Orchid
(O. sphegodes ssp. atrata)

    Long classified as a subspecies of *Ophrys sphegodes* or "Early Spider Orchid", *Ophrys incubacea* is now regarded as a species in its own right, but has been retained in the complex "Sphegodes group" of very closely related species – all with flowers somewhat reminiscent of spiders.

    Indeed, dark-hued, rotund and hairy as its lip is, *Ophrys incubacea*, from a distance, might well be mistaken for such an insect, poised amid foliage, its beady eyes intently watching out for some unwitting prey.

Ophrys incubacea varies in size from about 15 to 30 cm. The basal leaves are spread out and 2 or 3 upper leaves, reduced in size, sheathe the stem.

The inflorescence is lax, consisting of 2 to 8 flowers, with green bracts longer than the stalk-like ovary.

The 3 sepals, generally broadly oval, are yellowish green and bear a conspicuous darker vein, the lateral sepals outspread, the median erect. The 2 smaller petals, oblong and with slightly wavy edge, are an orangey green and often have a thin orangey to purplish red margin.

The lip, up to 1.5cm in length, is broad and usually rounded, its ground colour a deep purplish brown or maroon. It is 3-lobed, the side lobes taking the form of hump-like protuberances, thickly hairy as are the margins of the middle lobe.

The "speculum" is variable and consists of blue markings on a glabrous background – two parallel stripes, separate or joining to form a vague H with very short upper parts.

Flowering: March – April

Habitat: An uncommon species, it is occasionally found on grassy, stony hillsides and in grassy clearings among pinewoods.

Name: For the generic name *Ophrys*, see *Ophrys fusca*, p. 36. While the epithet *atrata* referred to the very dark colour of this plant's flowers, the meaning of *incubacea* is less clear – and may refer to the somewhat "oblique" position of the flowers on the stem, although, depending on the interpretation of the Latin word, it may simply point to the small size of the plant.

Ophrys speculum   Mirror Orchid
(O. ciliata, O. vernixia)

Given its size, *Ophrys speculum* may be regarded as a humble plant. But there is nothing humble about its sophisticated flowers, which may not be beautiful in the accepted sense, yet never fail to arouse a feeling of wonder ... For, with a "mirror" as blue as a summer sky, a shaggy fringe of hairs the colour of the dye henna, a head – half hidden – with gaping mouth and bulging eyes, they look less like flowers than creatures of the science fiction world ready to spring to life! There is no doubt about it, *Ophrys speculum* is a truly amazing little plant!

Ophrys speculum is a small plant in the 10-15 cm bracket, with leaves forming a basal rosette and 1 to 3, reduced in size, sheathing the stem.

The inflorescence is lax, comprising 2 to 8 flowers, with greenish bracts longer than the stalk-like ovary.

Of the 3 greenish sepals, the 2 lateral, purple-veined or widely striped, are spread horizontally, while the curly-edged median curves forward over the column.

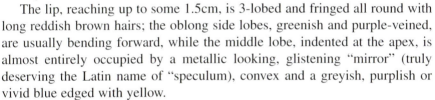

The 2 petals, purplish brown and velvety, look small and blunt, due to the fact that the tips are recurved.

The lip, reaching up to some 1.5cm, is 3-lobed and fringed all round with long reddish brown hairs; the oblong side lobes, greenish and purple-veined, are usually bending forward, while the middle lobe, indented at the apex, is almost entirely occupied by a metallic looking, glistening "mirror" (truly deserving the Latin name of "speculum), convex and a greyish, purplish or vivid blue edged with yellow.

Flowering:	Mid-March to May.
Habitat:	*Ophrys speculum* is found with other "Bee Orchids" in open pinewoods and on grassy hillsides. It also grows on uncultivated terraces.
Name:	For the generic name *Ophrys*, see *O. fusca* p. 36.
	The specific name refers to the "mirror" central to the lip – a major feature of the species, also recalled in the popular English name.
	Another name, *ciliata* (from the Latin *cilium*, meaning "eyelashes"), while evocative of the hairy fringe around the lip of the flower, refers to the insect commonly pollinating the flowers (see "Note" below).
Note:	Botanists, including Charles Darwin, puzzled over the resemblance of Ophrys flowers to insects without finding a suitable explanation, until a Frenchman named Pouyanne discovered the process of their pollination after studying *O. speculum* flowers and their close association with the small wasp *Campsoscolia ciliata*.

Orchis olbiensis   Little Early Purple Orchid
(O. mascula ssp. olbiensis)

Long, and by some, still considered a subspecies of *Orchis mascula* or "Early Purple Orchid", this slender plant of the West Mediterranean region occurs quite commonly in Mallorca, where it seems to thrive especially on well exposed grassy mountain slopes, climbing as high as 1300 m or so.

While it cannot boast the height of sturdy *Orchis mascula*, *Orchis olbiensis* easily makes up for its smaller size by the delicate colouring of its graceful flowers, besides lacking the unpleasant smell, supposedly reminiscent of cat urine, which its close relative exhales!

Orchis oibiensis is a plant of about 10 to 25 cm or more in height, with basal leaves sometimes purple-spotted and upper leaves, reduced in size, sheathing the stem. The inflorescence is a lax spike, comprising 5 to 12 spurred flowers, more on occasion, with pink to purplish bracts often shorter than the twisted stalk-like ovary. The 3 sepals are pale to purplish pink, the 2 lateral erect, the median curving forward to form, together with the 2 smaller petals, a hood over the column. The lip, 1,2cm long or more, is 3-lobed with a pale purple-spotted central band. The side lobes, white to pink with a slightly wavy edge, are more or less reflexed, while the middle lobe, longer, is indented at the apex, with a tiny tooth in the centre. The purplish spur curves upwards; longer than the ovary, it is enlarged towards the tip.

Flowering: March – April
Habitat: This plant favours grassy areas on limestone and is mainly found on sunny hillsides and mountain slopes
Name: For the generic name *Orchis*, see *Orchis conica*, p. 42.
The species derives its name from *Olbia*, the ancient name of Hyeres, in the south of France.
Note: *Orchis mascula*, of which *O. olbiensis* used to be classified as a subspecies, was one of the main Orchids commercially exploited until relatively recently, as its tubers were used to make up the beverage of Middle Eastern origin known as Sahlep (or Salep), reputed for its nutritious properties.
The tubers were also believed to be widely used by witches in their love philtres – the new tuber serving to foster true love, the old, shrunken tuber helping to thwart undesired or undesirable passions.

Ophrys lutea   Yellow Bee Orchid

Ophrys lutea may not be classified by all experts among the rarest Mallorcan Orchids, yet it is a rather elusive plant, for it seems to grow in very localised colonies, added to which, as is the case with many Orchids, it does not always reappear from one year to the next unless conditions are optimal.

Hence, much time may be spent criss-crossing garrigue areas carpeted with flowers and pine woods where Rosemary spreads a haze of mauve ... all to no avail! Which makes discovery, of course, all the more exciting, especially as *Ophrys lutea* boasts charming flowers which flaunt a bright yellow lip where some dark insect, its glossy wings folded, seems to have settled.

Ophrys lutea is usually a small plant, rarely exceeding 20 cm in height. The basal leaves form a rosette and the upper leaves, reduced in size, sheathe the stem. The inflorescence consists of 2 to 8 flowers (occasionally more) in a lax spike, with green bracts longer than the ovary serving as stalk.

The 3 sepals are green, the 2 lateral broad and "cupped", the median, with curling edges, curving forward. The 2 petals, much shorter and narrowly oblong, are a yellowish green, and the wavy edge is often tinged with orange.

The large lip – about 1.8cm by 1.5cm – is arched at the base and has a broad yellow margin. It is 3-lobed, the side lobes wide and spreading, the middle lobe, equally wide, indented at the apex.

The "speculum", on a dark brown patch reminiscent in shape and colour of O. fusca, consists of bluey-grey markings forming a 2-lobed pattern.

Flowering: March – April
Habitat: *Ophrys lutea* is apparently found in garrigue and maquis as well as in grassy areas in pinewoods (more particularly in the island's northern region).
Name: For the generic name *Ophrys*, see *Ophrys fusca* p. 36. *"lutea"*, the Latin word for "golden yellow" refers to the brilliant hue of the lip of the flower.

Orchis italica   Italian or Naked Man Orchid

Popular names of plants are often more descriptive and less inhibited than their scientific counterparts. They aim at conveying instant images to the mind – and *Orchis italica*, with its popular English name "The Naked Man Orchid" is a case in point ... For there is no doubt about the sex of the tiny figures which the flowers masquerade as: every twisting and turning member of this lively ballet is obviously a man, unashamedly naked! With such flowers, and crinkly-edged dark-spotted leaves that are very handsome, *Orchis italica* is an easy plant to recognise, and the small colonies it forms are a striking sight. Unfortunately, it is not a common plant and its distribution tends to be localised.

Orchis italica is a plant of variable size, at times reaching more than 30 cm in height. The basal leaves are rosetted while the upper leaves, reduced in size, sheathe the stem. The inflorescence consists of a dense spike (up to 15cm in length) of white to pink flowers with a down-pointing spur and membranous bracts shorter than the twisted stalk-like ovary.

The 3 long pointed sepals, white or pink and purple-veined, curve forward to form, together with the 2 smaller petals a protective hood over the column.

The lip, 1,5 to 2cm or more in length, is often a deeper hue than the sepals and petals and is very deeply 3-lobed. The side lobes, long, thin and pointed at the tip, are spreading and often twisted, as are the two segments of the middle lobe. Between the latter, there is a pointed appendage of variable length. Hence, the impression of little male figures with arms and legs in motion.

Flowering:	Mid-March to late April.
Habitat:	*Orchis italica* favours limestone and is mainly found, very locally, in grassy patches of garrigue and in clearings or along the edge of pinewoods.
Name:	For the generic name *Orchis*, see *Orchis conica*, p. 42. The epithet *"italica"* indicates the area, Italy, from which this species was first identified.

Ophrys balearica   Balearic Bee Orchid
(O. bertolonii, O. bertoloniiformis)

Ophrys balearica is a new "discovery", at least as far as nomenclature is concerned. The plant first appeared in works on the Balearic Islands as *O. bertolonii* – the latter being regarded as a plant with a range extending from southern France to beyond Yugoslavia. Following further studies, the distribution of *O. bertolonii* was seen as restricted to the eastern part of the Mediterranean, and the closely resembling species present in the western region was given the name of *O. bertoloniiformis*.

However, the very latest research points to the fact that the Orchid found in the Balearic Islands possesses sufficient individual features to be classified as an endemic plant, hence the new specific name it has received.

The species probably evolved from the hybridisation of *O. bertolonii* and *O. incubacea* and is quite common in Mallorca. With the velvety darkness of their lip enhanced by the pink hue of sepals and petals, and with their bird-like profile and often striking shape – as of an insect on its back striving to get away – the flowers are extremely attractive.

O. balearica is a sturdy plant, generally from 15 to 35 cm in height, with basal leaves in a rosette and upper leaves, reduced in size, sheathing the stem.

The inflorescence is a lax spike of 6 to 8 flowers at the most, with green bracts longer than the stalk-like ovary.

The 3 sepals are pink, sometimes very pale, with the base a deeper shade and a prominent green central vein; the 2 petals, oblong or somewhat triangular, are often a deeper pink and slightly wavy-edged. The 2 lateral sepals and the 2 petals are outspread, while the raised median sepal curves forward.

The lip, which may reach some 2 cm in length, is densely hairy and of velvety appearance; it is a very dark brown, somewhat lighter and more maroon at the edges; generally 3lobed – with the indented middle lobe bearing an up-curving bright greenish yellow appendage – the lip may be slightly depressed in the centre, but not arched and saddlelike as is *O. bertolonii*.

The small "speculum", entire and shield-like or divided in two, varies from greyish blue to purple and may be outlined in white. Two prominent dots, green with dark centres gleam, eye-like, at the side of the stigmatic cavity.

Flowering: From mid/late March to May.
Habitat: This plant is not uncommon and is generally found – on limestone – along forest margins and tracks, in open pinewoods and on grassy hillsides, also, occasionally, on disused terraces.
Name: For the generic name *Ophrys* see *Ophrys fusca* p. 36.
O. bertolonii was named after the Italian botanist Antonio Bertoloni (1775 – 1869). The new specific name, *"balearica"*, given to this Ophrys by the Belgian botanist Pierre Delforge, points, of course, to the endemic nature of the plant.

Serapias lingua   Tongue Orchid

Serapias are not, perhaps, plants one easily takes to. In fact, chancing upon them, one may well be tempted to dismiss them without more ado, for they are not impressive in size and their strange flowers (which may not always be immediately recognised as such) are not particularly appealing either in shape or colour.

Dull as they seem, however, these little plants are well worthy of a closer look. Then, their originality is revealed, the geometry of their profile noticed.... With their vertical bract, their elongated, almost horizontal, hood and that long, pointed, hanging tongue complete with "taste buds", *Serapias* are far from insignificant!

Serapias lingua is a slender plant, 10 to 25 cm tall, with leaves somewhat channelled and long-pointed sheathing the stem, which is often red or purple-spotted.

The inflorescence consists of a spike comprising few flowers arranged almost at right angle to the stem. The bracts, a dull purplish pink with darker veins, long-pointed and erect, enclose the ovary.

The 3 sepals and 2 thinner petals, similar to the bracts in colour or slightly paler, form an elongated quasi-horizontal hood over the column.

The lip, some 2cm long, is 3-lobed. The side lobes, hidden within the hood, are a deep purple, rounded and curving upwards; the middle lobe is shaped like a pointed tongue, the colour varying from pale orangey yellow to purplish red. It is hairy towards the base – where tiny insects get caught – and bears minute protuberances. At the base, a prominent hump, dark-hued and singly furrowed, may be observed.

Flowering: From mid/late March to May.

Habitat: An apparently accommodating species, *Serapias lingua* is found in various terrain, in grassy damp areas and on dry stony hillsides, in pine woods as well as in maquis. It tends to form colonies, which may be quite dense.

Name: This plant was given the name of the Egyptian god *Serapias* – associated with a fertility cult – perhaps through a confusion with another Orchid reputed as an aphrodisiac. However, the tradition is ancient and the Latin author Pliny already refers to Tongue Orchids as Serapias.

The specific name (Latin *"lingua"*) recalls the resemblance of the lip of these plants to the "tongue".

Serapias parviflora   Small-flowered Serapias

This plant grows in similar habitats to those favoured by *Serapias lingua* and is often found in its colonies. In fact, at a first glance, it may be taken just for a humbler version of its relative, for it bears flowers which, though smaller – as the specific name indicates – seem very close in appearance.

Close, they certainly are, yet sufficiently different to warrant a distinct status.

The leaves, more deeply channelled, are often red-spotted at the base and the lax floral spike is not so strikingly "geometrical" as the flowers tend to align more closely with the bracts.

The lip is 3-lobed. The side lobes, very dark and erect, are hidden within the hood; the middle lobe, orangey to brownish red and resembling a narrow, long-pointed tongue, is sharply reflexed; the hairy base bears 2 dark humps.

Serapias parviflora may vary in colouring: sepals and petals, usually a dull pink, are not always veined; they may be greenish, in which case the "tongue" is a pale yellowish hue.

Biniaraix

Neotinea maculata   Dense-flowered Orchid
(Neotinea intacta)

Wandering through Mallorcan maquis in the spring, at a time when broom and cistus shrubs are still in full bloom and whole hillsides are ablaze with colour, it is easy to miss the flowering spikes of *Neotinea maculata* hidden in the midst of dense vegetation and often in the shade. And when discovered, the first reaction may be to disregard the pale flowers as of little interest, for they are minute and only through magnification can they be properly observed and appreciated.

Neotinea maculata is a slender plant rarely exceeding 30 cm in height, with relatively large leaves, a bluey green and plain or purple-spotted, the basal leaves spreading, the upper leaves decreasing in size and finally sheathing the stem.

The inflorescence is a compact spike of small, fragrant flowers, mainly turned to one side, with short bracts about as long as the stalk-like ovary.

The flowers may be a variable pink or a greenish white – in which case the leaves are unspotted. The 3 sepals and 2 petals form a rather disproportionate hood with regard to the lip, a few millimetres long, which is 3-lobed and reminiscent in shape of a long armed human figure.

The spur is very short.

Flowering:	Late March to mid-May.
Habitat:	*Neotinea maculata* favours chalky soils, but also tolerates some acidity. It is mainly found in maquis and on grassy rocky slopes, climbing to the 1000 m line and beyond. It seems to do well in both sun and shade.
Name:	The genus Neotinea, which comprises a single species, owes its name to a XIXth century Sicilian botanist, V.Tineo.
	The Latin word maculata refers to the "spotted" leaves, which characterise the pink flowered and most common form of the species.

Aceras anthropophorum — Man Orchid

Very similar to Orchids, but lacking their spur, *Aceras anthropophorum* readily associates with long grasses at the edge of woods or in mountain pastures, where its slender spikes of often pale flowers tend to blend with the background, and the little men they seem to mimic remain unheeded – little hanged men, that is, with their bare limbs and head sadly lolling, as if dislocated...

Aceras anthropophorum is a plant some 15 to 30 cm in height, with glossy leaves somewhat wavy edged and channelled, several spreading around the slender stem and a few, reduced in size, sheathing it.

The inflorescence consists of a long narrow spike of numerous yellowish flowers, spurless. The bracts, also yellowish, are shorter than the twisted ovary serving as stalk. The 3 sepals and 2 petals, yellowish (or greenish) red-veined and conspicuously red edged, curve forward to form a large hood over the column.

The lip, between 1 and 1,5 cm long, is 3-lobed, with the side lobes long and narrow and the middle lobe divided, thus giving the impression of a man's arms and legs – the colour of which may vary from greenish yellow to orangey red.

At the base of the lip are 2 small humps with, in between, a cavity where nectar accumulates.

Flowering: Late March to June.
Habitat: This plant often grows in the longer grass and favours sunny areas on limestone, though it may also be found in the shade among pine trees.
Name: As this Orchid is the only species in the genus, the name *Aceras* applies to both and points to the difference between true Orchids and this plant, which is (literally translated from the Greek), "without a horn", i.e. without a spur. Also derived from the Greek, the epithet *anthropophorum*, meaning "man-bearing", points to the appearance of the flower.

Orchis fragrans* var. *martrinii   Fragrant Bug Orchid
(O. coriophora ssp. fragrans)

Unlike the "Bug Orchid" (*Orchis coriophora*) which owes its name to the odour it exhales, supposedly reminiscent of bedbugs (a tribute to the olfactory sensitivity of past botanists), the closely related *Orchis fragrans* (still considered by some specialists as a subspecies of *O. coriophora*) is definitely sweet-scented, thus fully deserving the epithet of "fragrant". The variety (or subspecies, for some) found in Mallorca is quite a sturdy plant, often boasting unusually colourful flowers which, seen in profile, suddenly turn into tiny birds with long sharp bills, perched along the stem in orderly fashion.

Orchis fragrans var. *martrinii* is a plant reaching some 35 cm in height, with rather narrow, channelled leaves, some of which, reduced in size, sheathe the stem. The inflorescence consists of a dense spike of spurred flowers, with pale green-veined bracts about the same length as the stalk-like ovary. The 3 sepals, pinkish flushed a deep red and with elongated tips, form, together with the 2 petals, a long-pointed hood over the column.

The lip, 1cm or more in length, varies in colour from pinkish to dark red and has a paler spotted central patch at the base. It is 3-lobed, the middle lobe longer and narrower than the outspread side lobes.

The sturdy spur points downwards.

Flowering: April – May
Habitat: Growing on soils rich in limestone, this plant likes damp areas or areas where humidity is high during the winter. Not particularly common in the island, it may be found near marshes as well as on grassy hillsides or among maquis undergrowth.
Name: For the generic name *Orchis*, see *Orchis conica* p. 42. The Latin *"fragrans"* characterises this sweet-smelling species.

Orchis robusta   Marsh Loose-flowered Orchid
(Orchis laxiflora ssp. palustris)

Orchis robusta may be said to be the pride and joy of Mallorca, for not only is it the most impressive Orchid species to be found in the region, but one of the rarest, growing as it does only in one or two restricted areas in the marshland of S'Albufera, the Nature Reserve in the north of the island.

Hiding behind a thick screen of towering reeds and surrounded by uninviting soggy terrain, this plant provides a real challenge for the Orchid hunter ... But what a thrill when, after a long quest, it is discovered at last – in small colonies, whose tall flowering spikes vividly glow against the backdrop of sun-dappled reed canes, and whose flowers are a delight to look at, so like miniature flying angels, complete with uplifted wings and wind-blown robes!

A slender looking plant, *Orchis robusta* may reach more than 80 cm in height and has long, narrow leaves, channelled and long-pointed, the upper leaves, reduced in size, sheathing the stem almost to the inflorescence.

The inflorescence consists of a somewhat lax spike – up to 20 cm long ~ of spurred pink to purplish pink flowers, with dark-veined greenish-purplish bracts longer than the twisted stalk-like ovary.

Of the 3 sepals, the 2 lateral are usually raised while the median curves forward to form, together with the 2 petals, a hood over the column.

The wide lip varies from pale to bright purplish pink with the central part paler and pink-spotted. It is 3-lobed, the side lobes, wide and with irregularly toothed edges, outspread or almost folded back, the median lobe indented at the apex.

The spur, with a slightly tapering tip, may be horizontal or pointing downwards.

Flowering:	Mid-April to late May.
Habitat:	This species is only present in the marshes of S'Albufera in the north of the island.
Name:	For the generic name *Orchis*, see *Orchis conica* p. 42. The Latin word *robusta* refers to the size and sturdiness of this handsome plant

Ophrys apifera   Bee Orchid

This is the Ophrys which gave the whole genus its popular English name of "Bee Orchid", for the small flowers of *Ophrys apifera* have long assumed – whether in shape, colour or texture – the appearance of the insects which used to pollinate them.

For some reason, however, this plant has practically ceased to rely on insect pollination and is the only Ophrys to resort to self-pollination, allowing the "pollinia" (or pollen masses) to slide out of their envelopes at an early stage and, thanks to their flexible "caudicles" (or stalks) touch and adhere to the stigmatic surface, with the result, it seems, that signs of degenerescence are appearing.

Still, degenerating or not, the little flowers, with their bright hues and sinuous profile, remain enchanting.

Ophrys apifera is a plant greatly varying in size, according to the location and prevailing conditions, from 15 to about 40 cm, with basal leaves in a rosette and upper leaves, reduced in size, sheathing the stem.

The inflorescence is a lax spike of relatively few flowers – 3 to 10 – with green bracts generally longer than the stalk-like ovary. The 3 large sepals, green-veined and varying from white to carmine pink, are outspread, as are the 2 small, downy petals, greenish or pink and almost triangular in shape.

The lip is small, about 1cm in length, a deep velvety brown. It is 3-lobed: the side lobes are prominent, hump-like, triangular in shape, hairy and with reflexed margins; the middle lobe, also with reflexed margins, is rounded, with a small appendage at the apex in-turned.

The "speculum" is variable, usually vaguely reminiscent of a widely opened W, a reddish or purplish brown, surrounded by a whitish or yellowish border. Below, two bright yellow dots may be seen, sometimes separately linked to the "speculum" by a thin line.

The column is elongated, with a characteristic sinuous projection.

Flowering: April to June.
Habitat: *Ophrys apifera* may be found on grassy hillsides, in maquis and along wood margins. It also seems to do well in abandoned orchards and in terrain recently disturbed, such as new pine plantations.
Name: For the generic name *Ophrys*, see *Ophrys fusca* p. 36. Derived from two Latin words *apis* and *ferre*, meaning "carrying a bee", the specific name refers to the aspect of the flower as well as to its pollinator.

Limodorum abortivum   Violet Limodore

After a winter and early spring favoured with abundant rainfall, it is not unusual to encounter, at the foot of pine trees in the shady depths of woods, small clusters of tall sturdy shoots of a bright violet hue, bearing slim spikes of unexpectedly attractive flowers, where various shades of violet and mauve happily contrast with white and yellow. These are the flowering stems of *Limodorum abortivum* whose uncommon aspect – and size when conditions are propitious – make it an impressive and unmistakable plant.

The sturdy stem of *Limodorum abortivum*, which may reach 70 cm or more in height, has no green leaves surrounding its base, but is closely sheathed by purplish-brown scales.

The inflorescence consists of a lax spike of up to 20 spurred flowers, with purple veined bracts longer than the twisted stalk-like ovary.

The 3 sepals are violet with a whitish base, the 2 lateral outspread, the median "cupped" and curving forward over the column; the 2 petals, smaller, are also outspread.

The wide triangular lip has a central purple-veined white area and its purple, wavy edges are generally curled up.

The spur points downwards.

Flowering:	Late April to June
Habitat:	This plant is relatively common and is mainly found, close to pine trees, in woodland with a thick layer of humus.
Name:	The generic name *Limodorum* is apparently the Latinized form of the Greek name given to parasitic plants, probably "Broomrapes".
	The Latin epithet *abortivum* refers to the scales sheathing the stem, considered as "abortive" leaves.
Note:	*Limodorum abortivum* is regarded by most specialists as a "saprophyte", i.e. a plant which derives its nourishment from decaying matter, although others hold it to be "parasitic", i.e. directly obtaining its food from the roots of living plants.

Anacamptis pyramidalis   Pyramidal Orchid

Though fond of sheltering among the grass on sunny hillsides or in open woodland, handsome *Anacamptis pyramidalis* cannot remain long unnoticed, for the perfect cone of the new inflorescence and the bright pink of the flowers never fail to attract attention. As more flowers open, the cone lengthens, losing its typical shape in the process, but by then the interest centres on the dense, striking form of the inflorescence and on the flowers themselves spreading wide all their colourful "limbs", all the better, it seems, to welcome and hug some hovering butterfly – a potential pollinator.

Anacamptis pyramidalis is a slender plant which may reach some 50 cm in height, with unspotted long-pointed leaves, the basal leaves spread out, the upper, reduced in size until scale-like, sheathing the stem.

The inflorescence is a spike, at first pyramidal, then cylindrical, densely grouping spurred flowers of various shades of pink, with purplish-pink bracts as long as the stalk-like ovary.

Of the 3 pink sepals, the 2 lateral are outspread, while the median curves forward to form, together with the 2 petals, a hood over the column.

The lip, some 8mm long, pink with a paler central patch, is deeply cut into 3 lobes, the side lobes outspread, the middle lobe with a small point at the apex. At the base of the lip 2 prominent ridges may be seen.

The spur, long and thin, curves downwards.

Flowering:	Late March to June
Habitat:	*Anacamptis pyramidalis* mainly grows on calcareous soils or marl. Favouring a dry, sunny environment, it also shows a preference for long grass. It often forms large colonies in open pine woods along the seashore or at the edge of maquis, also on well exposed hillsides. It is found in the island up to about 1000 m.
Name:	The name *Anacamptis* given to the genus, of which the present plant is the only representative, is derived from two Greek words meaning "bent back" and refers to the shape of the spur. The specific name *pyramidalis* obviously refers to the shape of the new inflorescence.
Note:	The two ridges at the base of the lip leave a narrow channel between them only suitable for the proboscis of a butterfly or moth to thread its way to the nectar stored in the long down-curving spur. In the process, the insect collects on its proboscis the pollinia (or pollen masses) which will serve to pollinate another *Anacamptis flower*.

Anacamptis pyramidalis var. albiflora

This pretty variety, bearing delicate white flowers, is not uncommon and may be found in small separate colonies or happily mixing with its pink-flowered relatives.

Cephalanthera longifolia — Sword-leafed Helleborine

Against a background of dense undergrowth or in the shadowy depths of a holm-oak wood, these plants, caught in a ray of sunlight, are a surprising sight, so fresh is the green of their glistening leaves and so brilliant the pure white of their dainty flowers – that can only be recognised as Orchid flowers, when they open fully and spread their fragile "wings" ... Which they are not always prepared to do.

Cephalanthera longifolia is a plant varying in size from 20 to 40 cm or so, with numerous lanceolate leaves up the stem, which may vary from broad to narrow, hence previously giving rise to different varieties – *latifolia* or "broad-leaved" and *angustifolia* or narrow-leafed

The inflorescence consists of a fairly dense spike of spurless white flowers with very short bracts, thus leaving exposed the twisted ovary, erect and truly stalk-like. The 3 sepals and 2 petals, about the same length, may form, together with the lip, a kind of half-closed bell, or the lateral sepals and lip may be partially spreading. The lip, less than 1 cm in length, is divided into 2 parts by a constriction in the middle : the forepart, with a tongue-like tip and upturned margins, bears several orange ridges which are said to secrete nectar. The basal part, concave, bears an orangey mark.

Flowering: Late April to June.
Habitat: Although it may be found in sunny places, *Cephalanthera longifolia* seems to prefer the coolness and shade of woodland, where it is not abundant, but may occasionally be seen, often in small clusters, around oak or pine trees.
Name: Derived from the Greek *kephale* (head) and modern Latin *anthem* (anther), the name given to the genus seems to refer to the protruding male organs "head-like". *Longifolia* from two Latin words, characterises the species as "long-leafed".
Note: The texture of sepals and petals, particularly brilliant and light reflecting, would seem especially adapted to render the plants more conspicuous to insect pollinators in the shadowy surroundings of woodland.

Cephalanthera damasonium

Perhaps more common in Mallorca than the preceding species and found in similar habitats, the "White Helleborine" is distinguished by its oval-shaped leaves spirally arranged around the stem, its inflorescence with long bracts and creamy flowers, larger than those of *C. longifolia* but without their sparkle and generally remaining half-closed.

Epipactis microphylla — Small-leafed Helleborine

Of the large number of European species of *Epipactis*, only one – *E. microphylla* – now seems to grow in Mallorca, although the presence of the handsomer *E. helleborine* is mentioned in relatively recent botanical works.

Epipactis microphylla, not exactly abundant itself, is usually found in holm-oak forests, where its slender stems are not always easy to detect given the size and colour of the leaves and the overall dullness of the small flowers – which only reveal their intriguing features when fully open and closely observed.

Epipactis microphylla is a plant varying in height from 15 to 40 cm, with few very small leaves, sometimes purple-tinged, spirally arranged around the stem, which is densely glandular-hairy in the upper part and often bent.

The inflorescence is a lax spike comprising up to 15 flowers or so, small, fragrant, grey-green tinged with pink and externally hairy. They are noticeably stalked and tend to droop to one side when in bud. The bracts decrease in size, the inferior longer than the ovary, the superior shorter. The ovary is not twisted.

The 3 sepals, greenish with purple veins, are "cupped" and, curving forward, form, together with the 2 pinkish petals, a kind of bell. Sepals and petals are rarely fully outspread.

The pale lip, 5 to 6mm long, is divided into two parts by a constriction in the middle: the forepart is heart-shaped and bears conspicuous humps, deeply crinkled, frill-like; the basal part is shallowly concave and has pink edges.

There is no spur.

Flowering: May – June

Habitat: This plant, fond of shade, is a woodland species. In the island, it is mainly found in holm-oak forests where there is little undergrowth.

Name: Derived from a Greek word meaning "coagulate", the generic name *Epipactis* apparently refers to the effect of these plants on milk, causing it to curdle.

This particular plant is characterised by its "small leaves", hence the specific name derived from the two corresponding Greek words: *micro* and *phylla*.

Neottia nidus-avis   Bird's Nest Orchid

Faced, for the first time and unprepared, with those sickly spears, reminiscent of asparagus, clustered at the foot of trees in deep forest land, one may well wonder what strange plants these can be. Parasites like "Broomrape" perhaps?

With one or two flowers open, however, there can be no doubt about it : those dull looking plants are obvious members of the Orchid family ... A startling discovery! The flowers of *Neottia nidus-avis* also come as a complete surprise, for they are quite remarkable, boasting as they do well-formed helmeted little figures – clown-like with their upturned legs – which suddenly gleam a burnished gold when caught in a ray of sunshine.

Some 30 to 40 cm in height, *Neottia nidus-avis* is a leafless plant, except for a few brown scales sheathing the lower part of the sturdy stem.

The inflorescence is spike-like, pyramidal at first then cylindrical, and comprises pale brownish fragrant flowers, quite densely packed. The bracts are shorter than the ovary, which is not twisted and is borne on a very short pedicel.

The 3 sepals are thinly, sparsely purplish-veined with the median somewhat wider and shorter than the lateral; they curve forward to form, together with the petals, a loose rounded hood over the column, of which the bright yellow pollinia are conspicuous. The lip, about 1cm in length, is 3-lobed, with the side lobes hardly developed and the middle lobe deeply

divided – the rounded segments widely apart and upturned. Bead like nectar secretions may be seen towards the base of the lip, while the underside is covered with glandular hairs, as is the ovary.

There is no spur.

Flowering:	May – June.
Habitat:	This plant needs deep humus and likes shady places. It is mainly found, in the island, in the thick layer of dead leaves covering the ground in holm-oak forests.
Name:	Both the generic name *Neottia* and the specific name nidus-avis, meaning "bird's nest", refer to the tangled root system which characterises this plant.
Note:	*Neottia nidus-avis* is a saprophytic plant, deriving its nourishment from decomposed vegetable matter, in association with fungi located in its roots. This extraordinary plant, although visited by small flies, mainly relies on self-pollination. It is apparently able, if need be, to flower, pollinate itself and produce seeds underground!

Rare Orchids
present or reported present in Mallorca

As has been mentioned in the Introduction, other Orchids may be found in Mallorca, but they are extremely rare and usually so highly localised as to make their discovery problematic without a competent guide or, at least, previous knowledge of their habitats, while searching for them may also involve lengthy and arduous walks through mountainous terrain.

They are the following species

Cephalanthera rubra: Red Helleborine
    Habitat: mountains, among Holm-oaks
Limodorum trabutianum: Trabut's Violet Limodore
    Habitat: mountains, among Holm oaks
Gymnadenia conopsea: Fragrant Orchid
    Habitat: mountain pastures, above 800 m

Gymnadenia conopsea

Orchis papilionacea

Orchis simia

Ophris scolopax

Orchis papilionacea: Butterfly Orchid
   Habitat: garrigue in the plain
Orchis simia: Monkey Orchid
   Habitat: mountain garrigue, up to 500 m or so
Orchis collina: Fan-lipped Orchid
   Habitat: garrigue in the plain
Orchis mascula: Early Purple Orchid
   Habitat: mountain garrigue
Orchis spitzelii: Spitzel's Orchid
   Habitat: mountain garrigue above 1000 m
Ophrys insectifera: Fly Orchid
   Habitat: pine woods, grassy areas
Ophrys scolopax: Woodcock Orchid
   Habitat: garrigue, up to some 800 m

Yet other Orchid species are mentioned in botanical works as present in Mallorca, but while their mention is sometimes the result of confusion between species, it is more often due to the repetition of quotations from earlier sources.

WILD ORCHIDS OF MALLORCA

PART III

APROXIMATE FLOWERING TIMES

Plant Names	J	F	M	A	M	J	J	A	S	O	N	D
Aceras anthropophorum				―	―	―						
Anacamptis pyramidalis				―	―	―						
Barlia robertiana			―	―								
Cephalanthera damasonium					―	―						
Cephalanthera longifolia					―	―						
Epipactis microphylla					―	―	―					
Gymnadenia conopsea						―	―					
Limodorum abortivum					―	―						
Neotinea maculata			―	―								
Neottia nidus-avis					―	―						
Ophrys apifera					―	―						
Ophrys balearica				―								
Ophrys bombyliflora			―	―								
Ophrys dyris				―								
Ophrys fusca	―	―	―								―	―
Ophrys incubacea				―	―							
Ophrys iricolor				―								
Ophrys lutea				―	―							
Ophrys speculum				―	―							
Ophrys tenthredinifera				―	―							
Orchis conica			―	―								
Orchis fragrans var. martrinii					―	―						
Orchis italica			―	―								
Orchis lactea			―	―								
Orchis longicornu			―	―								
Orchis olbiensis			―	―								
Orchis robusta				―								
Serapias lingua				―	―							
Serapias parviflora				―	―							
Spiranthes spiralis									―	―		

MAIN CHARACTERISTICS OF ORCHID GENERA FOUND IN MALLORCA

Epipactis (Helleborines : 1 species in Mallorca)

Plants of variable size, rhizomatous, leafy stem.
Inflorescence a lax spike of stalked flowers tending to droop; green bracts.
Flowers greenish purplish in the case of E. microphylla sepals and petals forming loose hood; lip divided by constriction into two parts: hypochile (basal part) concave, epichile (forepart) with pointed recurved tip; no spur; ovary not twisted
Column with conspicuous pollinia; no viscidia or bursicles; rostellum containing gluey substance.

Cephalanthera (White Helleborines : 3 species in Mallorca, 1 extremely rare)

Plants of variable size, rhizomatous; leafy stem,
Inflorescence a lax spike; green bracts.
Flowers white, cream (or pink); sepals and petals generally curving forward; lip divided by constriction into two parts: hypochile (basal part) concave, epichile (forepart) with recurved tip and longitudinal ridges at base; no spur; twisted stalk-like ovary.
Column with protruding pollinia; no viscidia or bursicles.

Limodorum (Violet Limodore : 2 species in Mallorca, 1 extremely rare)

Rhizomatous plants, generally regarded as saprophytic: tall stem, purple (or purplish green) sheathed with scales.
Inflorescence long, lax, spike-like; bracts purplish.
Flowers violet purple (or purplish); median sepal and petals forming hood or petals and lateral sepals outspread; lip triangular (or lanceolate); spur slender down-pointing (or very short); stalk-like ovary. Column with pollinia joined to single viscidium; no bursicle.

Neottia (Bird's Nest Orchid : single European species in genus)

Saprophytic plant of variable size, a pale brownish colour; rhizome with numerous roots in dense, tangled mass; 1 stem sheathed with few scales.

Inflorescence spike-like, dense, many-flowered; short bracts.
Flowers pale brownish; sepals and petals forming loose hood; lip 3-lobed, side lobes insignificant, median lobe divided; no spur; ovary with very short pedicel.
Column elongated; wide rostellum, flat; pollinia projecting without viscidia or bursicles.

Spiranthes (Lady's Tresses : 1 species in Mallorca)

Slender plants; tuberous roots; basal leaves rosetted in the case of S. spiralis.
Inflorescence a spirally twisted spike; green bracts; glandular hairs present.
Flowers fragrant, small, white in the case of S. spiralis, sepals and petals forming tubular hood; lip narrow with wavy edges; no spur; twisted stalk-like ovary.
Column horizontal; pollinia with single viscidium between bilobed rostellum.

Gymnadenia (Fragrant Orchids : 1 species in Mallorca, very rare)

Plants of variable size; 2 tubers; leafy stem.
Inflorescence a many-flowered spike; green bracts.
Flowers fragrant, pink in the case of G. conopsea ; median sepal and petals forming hood, lateral sepals often outspread; lip 3-lobed; spur very long and thin curving downwards; stalk-like ovary.
Column with long rostellum; pollinia with viscidia but no bursicles.

Neotinea (Dense-flowered Orchid : single species in genus)

Plant of variable size; 2 tubers; basal leaves rosetted, often purplish-spotted, upper leaves, reduced in size sheathing stem.
Inflorescence a very dense spike; short bracts.
Flowers very small, pink or white; sepals and petals forming hood; lip deeply 3-lobed; very short spur down-pointing; twisted stalk-like ovary.
Column with minute pollinia; viscidia in bilobed bursicle.

Orchis (Ground Orchids : 12 species in Mallorca, 5 extremely rare)

Plants greatly differing in size and appearance; 2 tubers; basal leaves spreading out or forming a rosette, upper leaves, generally reduced in size, sheathing stem.
Inflorescence a spike generally many-flowered; bracts usually coloured.
Flowers of various colours; sepals and petals forming hood or lateral sepals outspread; lip generally 3-lobed or with 4 lobes reminiscent of arms and legs of dangling figure; central area often paler and spotted; spur generally conspicuous; twisted stalk-like ovary.
Column with rostellum; pollinia with viscidia in bilobed bursicle.

Aceras (Man Orchid : single species in genus)

Slender plant; 2 tubers; glossy lanceolate leaves, basal leaves spreading out, upper leaves, reduced in size, sheathing stem.
Inflorescence a slim spike with numerous flowers; membranous bracts.

Flowers greenish to orangey yellow; sepals and petals forming hood; lip with 4 linear lobes; no spur; twisted stalk-like ovary.
Column, with compact pollinia; viscidia very close together in single bursicle.

Barlia (Giant Orchid : 1 species in Mallorca)

Tall, robust plant; 2 tubers; large glossy leaves, lanceolate, upper leaves, reduced in size, sheathing stem. Inflorescence a large, compact spike; very long lanceolate bracts.
Flowers fragrant, large, greenish pink (rarely whitish); sepals and petals forming loose hood; lip 3-lobed with divided middle lobe; short spur; twisted stalk-like ovary.
Column with pollinia joined to single viscidium in simple bursicle.

Anacamptis (Pyramidal Orchid : single species in genus)

Plant of variable size; 2 tubers; leaves narrow, lanceolate, basal leaves spreading out, upper leaves, reduced in size, sheathing stem.
Inflorescence a dense spike, pyramidal at first; small membranous bracts.
Flowers pale to bright pink; white variety; median sepal and petals forming hood, lateral sepals outspread; lip 3-lobed with 2 prominent ridges towards base; long, thin spur down-curving; twisted stalk-like ovary.
Column with small rostellum; pollinia joined to saddle-shaped viscidium in simple bursicle.

Serapias (Tongue Orchids : 2 species in Mallorca)

Slender plants; 2 tubers or more; leaves narrow, lanceolate, generally channelled, upper leaves, reduced in size, sheating stem.
Inflorescence a spike of generally few flowers; coloured bracts, long, lanceolate, usually cupped.
Flowers of variable reddish/pinkish hue; sepals, partially fused, forming long-pointed hood with petals; lip divided by constriction into two parts; hypochile (basal part) bilobed, usually hidden within hood; epichile (forepart) tongue-like; single or double hump at base of lip; no spur; stalk-like ovary. Flowers of S. parviflora sometimes with greenish sepals and petals and a yellowish lip.

Ophrys (Bee Orchids: 12 species in Mallorca, 2 extremely rare)

Generally smallish plants; 2 tubers; leaves usually broadly lanceolate, basal leaves in a rosette, upper leaves reduced in size generally sheathing stem.
Inflorescence usually a lax spike, often few-flowered; bracts lanceolate, green.
Flowers small; sepals – green, pink or almost white – the lateral sepals outspread, the median often curving forward; petals smaller, variously coloured; lip relatively large, entire or 3-lobed, velvety or hairy in parts, with markings and colours resembling specific insect pollinators; characteristic glistening central area, known as speculum; often small appendage at apex; no spur; stalk-like ovary.
Column surmounted by projection with profile said to resemble duck's head; minute rostellum; stalked pollinia with viscidia in separate bursicles.

GLOSSARY

Alternate: of leaves growing at different levels on the two sides of stem.
Annual: of plants, which complete life cycle within a year.
Anther: part of stamen containing pollen.
Apex: tip of organ.
Appendage: addition to larger organ.
Basal: at foot of stem; borne near base.
Bilobed: with 2 lobes.
Bract: modified or reduced leaf usually present at base of flower.
Bursicle: in Orchids, small flap or pouch protecting sticky disc of pollinium (pollen mass), known as viscidium.
Calyx: collective grouping of sepals free or united.
Capsule: dry fruit of a plant which splits open to release seeds.
Caudicle: in Orchids, stalk connecting pollinium (pollen mass) to sticky disc known as viscidium.
Column: in Orchids, organ combining stigmas, style and stamen(s) into a single structure.
Corolla: collective grouping of petals free or united.
Entire: of leaves, without divisions or teeth.
Epichile: forepart of lip when the latter is divided into 2 sections by a constriction
Garrigue: (or Garigue): open type of vegetation characterised by low shrubs, often aromatic, with flourishing communities of herbaceous perennials, typical of the Mediterranean region.
Genus: (pl. genera): group of plants consisting of distinct but related species.
Glabrous: without hairs.
Habitat: environment in which a plant lives.
Herbaceous: of plants, leafy, non-woody.
Hybrid: plant, often infertile, resulting from cross between different species.
Hypochile: basal part of lip when the latter is divided into 2 sections by a constriction.
Inflorescence: flowering section of stem, arrangement of flowers on stem.
Labellum: in Orchids, modified third or lower petal – "landing platform" for insect pollinators.
Lanceolate: shaped like lance, i.e. tapering towards apex.
Lax: not tightly grouped together, spaced out.
Lip: see "labellum".

Lobe: division of an organ.
Maquis: dense type of vegetation characterised by tall shrubs and scattered trees, typical of the Mediterranean region.
Median: central, middle.
Membranous: thin, flexible, like membrane.
Monocotyledon: plant with a single seed leaf.
Mycorrhizal Association: association of fungi with seeds or roots of plants to their mutual benefit.
Nectar: sweet substance secreted by plants which attracts insects.
Oblong: of leaves with sides almost parallel.
Ovary: basal part of pistil where seeds are formed.
Ovule: part of ovary containing germ cell developing into seed following fertilisation.
Parasite: plant that obtains its food from another living plant to which it is attached.
Pedicel: stalk of single flower.
Perennial: plant that lives for more than 2 years, flowers in its second year and annually thereafter.
Perianth: non-reproductive organs of a flower consisting of an outer whorl of sepals and an inner whorl of petals.
Petal: in Orchids, one of the 3 inner perianth parts, including labellum or lip.
Photosynthesis: process by which plants transform light energy into chemical energy, manufacturing food sugars with the aid of chlorophyll.
Pistil: female reproductive organ of a flower comprising stigma, style and ovary.
Pollen: small grains containing male reproductive cells of flowering plants.
Pollination: act of transferring pollen onto stigma or stigmatic surface of a flower.
Pollinium: in Orchids, compact mass of pollen grains cohering together and transported as a single unit by insects in the process of pollination.
Recurved: curved backwards.
Reflexed: bent backwards or downwards.
Rhizome: perennial underground stem, creeping horizontally, bearing both roots and shoots.
Rosette: cluster of leaves radiating from base of stem.
Rostellum: in some Orchids, outgrowth above stigmatic cavity representing sterile third stigma.
Saprophyte: plant obtaining its food from decaying organic matter.
Sepal: in Orchids, one of the three outer perianth parts.
Sheathing: of leaves with lower part surrounding stem.
Species: basic unit of plant classification : group of closely related plants showing constant, distinct features from similar groups.
Speculum: iridescent patch or inset in lip of Ophrys flowers.
Spike: elongated cluster of flowers, stalkless or practically so.
Spur: tube-like extension of flower often containing nectar.
Stamen: one of the male reproductive organs consisting of an anther containing pollen grains borne on a stalk or filament.
Stigma: part of female organ on which pollen is deposited (adj. stigmatic).

Style: connective part between stigma and ovary.

Subspecies: group of plants within a species with some distinctive characteristics.

Taxonomy: classification of plants and animals.

Tuber: swollen underground portion of stem or root, formed annually, where food reserves are stored.

Viscidium: in Orchids, sticky disc joined to pollinium by stalk (caudicle), enabling it to adhere to insect pollinator and be transported to fertilise other flower.

Whorl: arrangement of organs arising at same level and forming a ring.

INDEX

PART I 7
Foreword 9
Introduction 13
  1. About Orchids 13
  2. General Characteristics of Terrestrial Orchids 14
     – The Plant 15
     – The Flower 16
  3. Pollination Process 19
  4. Life Cycle: from Seed to Seed 21
  5. Habitats 23
  6. Classification of Orchids 27
Conclusion 31

PART II. WILD ORCHIDS OF MALLORCA 33
Spiranthes spiralis 34
Ophrys fusca 36
Barlia robertiana 40
Orchis conica 42
Orchis lactea 44
Ophrys tenthredinifera 46
Orchis longicornu 48
Ophrys bombyliflora 50
Ophrys incubacea 52
Ophrys speculum 54
Orchis olbiensis 56
Ophrys lutea 58
Orchis italica 60
Ophrys balearica 62
Serapias lingua 64
Serapias parviflora 66

Neotinea maculata .... .68
Aceras anthropophorum .... .70
Orchis fragrans var. martrinii .... .72
Orchis robusta .... .74
Ophrys apifera .... .76
Limodorum abortivum .... .78
Anacamptis pyramidalis .... .80
Cephalanthera longifolia .... .83
Epipactis microphylla .... .86
Neottia nidus-avis .... .88
Rare Orchids present or reported present in Mallorca .... .90

PART III .... .93
Diagram of Flowering Seasons .... .95
Resume of Characteristics of Genera found in Mallorca .... .97
Glossary .... .101
Bibliography .... .105